Junior GIRL SCOUT®

LEADER GUIDE BOOK

Girl Scouts of the USA | 420 Fifth Avenue | New York, NY 10018

National President
Connie L. Matsui

National Executive Director
Marsha Johnson Evans

National Director, Membership, Program and Diversity Group
Sharon Woods Hussey

Director, Program Development
Harriet S. Mosatche, Ph.D.

Authors
Rosemarie Cryan, Toni Eubanks, Sheila K. Lewis, Harriet S. Mosatche, Ph.D., Donna Nye, Karen Unger

Contributor
The American Institute of Chemical Engineers

Acknowledgements
Director of Publishing, Suzanna Penn; Project Editor, Mikki Morrissette; Assistant Editor, Susan Brody; Manager, Creative Design and Production, Christina Cannard-Seward; Marie Kary-Gargiulo, Technical Assistant; Gerri Brown, Director of Sales and New Market Development; Linda LeShanna, Director of Trademark and Licensing; Mindi Rosenthal, Merchandise Manager; Daria Scala, Manager of NES Advertising

Illustration
Adam Hurwitz: 22, 40, 55, 58.

Photography
The Girl Scouts: Lori Adamski-Peek Cover, 5b, 6, 8, 10, 14, 18, 20b, 30, 32, 35, 38b, 44t,45t, 46t, 46m; Richard Blinkoff 15; George Kerrigan/ Digital Eyes 9, 11, 16#'s 1-20, 17, 19, 20t, 26, 27, 31,38t, 44b, 48bl, 48br. Corbis: Ray Gehman 54m; Michael Gore/Frank Lane Pictures/Corbis 41tr; Tim Thompson 41bl; Brian Vikander 41ml; Kevin Karp: 16 #21; Omni-Photo: Shelley Rotner 22; Peter Arnold,Inc.: Jodi Jacobson 57; Photo Researchers: Ken Lax 51; Renee Lynn 50b; Bruce Roberts 49t; Blair Seitz 24; PhotoEdit: Myrleen Cate 41bl, 50t; Deborah Davis 40tl; Jeff Greenberg 40b; Richard Hutchings 42; Felicia Martinez 54tl, 55; Michael Newman 48mr; A. Ramey 41mr; David Young-Wolff 41tl, 45b; The Image works: Eastcott/Momatiuk 40tr; James Marshall 40b, Tim reese 56; The Stock Market: Peter Beck 46b, 48tl; Jon Feingersh 47; LWA-Dann Tardif 5t; David Pollack 43.

Design
Adventure House, NYC

Inquiries related to the *Junior Girl Scout Leader Guide Book* should be directed to Membership, Program and Diversity, Girl Scouts of the USA, 420 Fifth Avenue, New York, N.Y. 10018-2798.

Photos on page 5 and 10 courtesy of Pilgrim of Newport, Long Beach, California.
Photos on pages 18, 20 and 46 courtesy of California State University, Long Beach, Earl Burns Miller Japanese Garden.
Photo on page 8 courtesy Blue Submarine, Long Beach, California.

Junior GIRL SCOUT® LEADER GUIDE BOOK

CONTENTS

Introduction

Sharing experiences with a group of 8 to 11-year-old girls will be fun and rewarding (if you're prepared).

Competent, compassionate, silly, giggly, energetic, shy, and enthusiastic—these adjectives and many others describe the girls in your Junior Girl Scout troop or group. One minute you may be laughing at their antics, stories, and spontaneity. Other times you may feel angry at their mischievousness, irresponsibility, or inability to behave appropriately.

Finding What You Need

The purpose of this book is to facilitate your role as a Junior Girl Scout leader. You can count on it, like a trusted friend, for the answers to your simplest to most complex questions. For example, you might ask: "What kind of ceremony should be planned for girls who earn the Girl Scout Bronze Award?" You can find that information in Section 1, which describes ceremonies for celebrating achievements and other milestones, along with describing the basics of Girl Scouting. Section 1 also contains information about the revised Junior Girl Scout resources—the *Junior Girl Scout Handbook* and the *Junior Girl Scout Badge Book.*

Perhaps you are wondering: What is the best way to organize a Girl Scout meeting? Section 2 illustrates the different systems of troop government and has tips on planning activities and meetings.

Perhaps you are thinking: The girls in my troop really enjoyed a science activity in Chapter 9 of the *Junior Girl Scout Handbook.*

What else can I do to capitalize on their enthusiasm? Section 3 of this book will provide the answers by offering ideas for trips, activities, discussion topics, and service projects that relate to the various topics covered in the handbook.

Another common question is how to handle a girl who misbehaves and disturbs troop meetings. For a discussion of this type of issue, you can read Section 4, which offers solutions to problems commonly encountered by Junior Girl Scout leaders. That section also gives an overview of the developmental characteristics of Junior Girl Scouts.

Or, you may ask: Which activities are sure to please every time? Those are included in Section 5 of this book.

One book can't do it all, so Section 6 directs you to other Girl Scout resources that will help you best serve the girls in your troop or group.

Being a Junior Girl Scout leader is an experience to treasure. You will learn and grow together with a group of eager, enthusiastic, excited, and sometimes exasperating girls who are caught between childhood and adolescence. These girls are seeking role models just like you to help them make decisions and learn new skills.

Basic Girl Scout Information

The principles contained in the Girl Scout Promise and Law, as well as the objectives highlighted in the program goals, provide the foundation for all the activities, projects, and experiences enjoyed by girls and adults in Girl Scouting. The breadth and depth of these values and goals make Girl Scouting different from other youth-serving organizations.

The Four Program Goals

Four program goals serve as the foundation for all the materials, activities, and initiatives that are developed under the auspices of Girl Scouting. They are as follows:

1. Girls will develop to their full potential.

Girl Scouting will:

- Foster girls' feelings of self-acceptance and unique self-worth.
- Promote girls' perception of themselves as competent, responsible, and open to new experiences and challenges.
- Offer girls opportunities to learn new skills.
- Encourage girls' personal growth.
- Allow girls to utilize and practice talents and abilities.

2. Girls will relate to others with increasing understanding, skill, and respect.

Girl Scouting will:

- Help girls develop sensitivity to others and respect for their needs, feelings, and rights.
- Promote an understanding and appreciation of individual, cultural, religious, and racial differences.
- Foster the ability to build friendships and working relationships.

The Girl Scout PROMISE

On my honor, I will try:
To serve God and my country,
To help people at all times,
And to live by the Girl Scout Law.

Promesa de las Girl Scouts

Por mi honor, yo trataré:
De servir a Dios, y a mi patria,
Ayudar a las personas en todo momento,
Y vivir conforme a la Ley de las Girl Scouts.

The Girl Scout LAW

I will do my best to be:
Honest and fair,
Friendly and helpful,
Considerate and caring,
Courageous and strong, and
Responsible for what
I say and do,
And to
respect myself and others,
respect authority,
use resources wisely,
make the world a better place, and
be a sister to every Girl Scout.

La Ley de las Girl Scouts

Yo me esforzaré a:
Ser honrada y justa,
Cordial y servicial,
Considerada y compasiva,
Valiente y fuerte, y
Responsable de lo que digo y hago,
Y a respetarme a mi misma y a los demás,
Respetar la autoridad,
Usar los recursos de manera prudente,
Hacer del mundo un lugar mejor, y
Ser hermana de cada una de las Girl Scouts.

3. Girls will develop a meaningful set of values to guide their actions and to provide the foundation for sound decision-making.

Girl Scouting will:

- Help girls develop meaningful values and ethics that will guide their actions.
- Foster an ability to make decisions that are consistent with girls' values and that reflect respect for the rights and needs of others.
- Empower girls to act upon their values and convictions.
- Encourage girls to reexamine their ideals as they mature.

4. Girls will contribute to the improvement of society through the use of their abilities and leadership skills, working in cooperation with others.

Girl Scouting will:

- Help girls develop concern for the well-being of their communities.
- Promote girls' understanding of how the quality of community life affects every member of society.
- Encourage girls to use their skills to work with others for the benefit of all.

Who Can Be a Girl Scout?

Any girl who is 5 through 17 years old or in kindergarten through the twelfth grade can become a Girl Scout in the United States. Girls of different races, backgrounds, and religious groups are welcome in Girl Scouting.

Brownie Girl Scouts
Ages 6, 7, 8 or
grades 1, 2, 3

Daisy Girl Scouts
Ages 5-6 or grades K, 1

The **5**

age levels in
Girl Scouting are:

Junior Girl Scouts
Ages 8, 9, 10, 11 or
grades 3, 4, 5, 6

Cadette Girl Scouts
Ages 11, 12, 13, 14 or
grades 6, 7, 8, 9

Senior Girl Scouts
Ages 14, 15, 16, 17 or
grades 9, 10, 11, 12

Being Safe

One of your major responsibilities as a Girl Scout leader is to provide for the safety of girls. To ensure that the same high standard of safety is met in councils around the country, GSUSA publishes a book called *Safety-Wise*.

To ensure the safety of Girl Scout troops and groups, each leader receives one copy of *Safety-Wise*. *Safety-Wise* provides the guidance you need to guide girls through experiences that are educationally sound and safe so that the well-being of every Girl Scout is protected and maintained. All program activities must meet the program standards and guidelines stated in *Safety-Wise*.

Planning an activity is a three-step process.

1. The first step is to read universal checkpoints in Chapter 7 of *Safety-Wise*. Then, turn to either the Table of Contents or the Index for page references that apply to the specific activity your group is planning.
2. Read the Step 2 Activity Checkpoints at the beginning of the chapter where the activity is located.
3. Read the Step 3 Activity Checkpoints for the specific activity you are planning. Important health and safety terms in Girl Scouting are defined in the book's glossary.

Girl Scout Program Standards

As a Girl Scout leader, you must be familiar with the 35 Girl Scout Program Standards in *Safety-Wise*. These standards describe how to put the principles of the Girl Scout program into practice and outline the necessary elements of a quality program experience. The standards also describe basic health and safety practices that provide for the well-being of girls in your group. Each standard is followed by specific guidelines that more fully illustrate what must be accomplished to meet each standard. Your Girl Scout council will provide assistance in interpreting and applying each of these standards.

Earning Awards

For 8-11 year olds, earning awards can be exciting. Other areas of their lives may not give girls the feelings of pride and accomplishment that come from completing a badge, service activity, or leadership project. Help girls choose the awards they would like to earn. Show them that the process used to earn the award is as valuable as the pin or badge they will receive.

▶ Encourage girls to take time to enjoy their activities rather than rush through them simply to accumulate lots of things to wear on their uniforms.

You can adapt activities when circumstances make it difficult for girls to complete them as written. For example, girls may be asked to visit a museum or historical site in order to complete a badge activity. If these types of places are not close to where your troop or group meet or live, then girls can get similar information on the Internet or they can visit a local historical society to fulfill the requirements.

A Court of Awards (for more information, look in the *Junior Girl Scout Handbook)* can be held to recognize the work the girls did in earning their badges, signs, or other insignia. Girls should take the lead in planning this ceremony with your help.

Junior Girl Scout Badges

The *Junior Girl Scout Badge Book* contains 104 badges that encourage girls to gain knowledge, learn and improve skills, explore careers, and make differences in their communities in a wide variety of areas—from home repair to the arts, from wildlife to sports, from the sciences to global awareness.

The Girl Scout Bronze Award

The Girl Scout Bronze Award is the highest award a Junior Girl Scout can earn. To receive a Girl Scout Bronze Award, a girl completes a project that shows that she understands and lives by the Girl Scout Promise and Law. The Girl Scout Bronze Award is new to the program for Junior Girl Scouts.

To earn the Girl Scout Bronze Award, girls will be asked to do the following:

- Earn two badges that are related to their final project.
- Complete one of the Girl Scout signs.
- Earn the Junior Aide Patch or the Junior Girl Scout Leadership Award or two of the following badges: "Girl Scouting in the USA," "Girl Scouting Around the World," "Girl Scouting in My Future," "Lead On."
- Complete a Girl Scout Bronze Award project.

A detailed explanation of these requirements appears in the *Junior Girl Scout Handbook.*

Sign of the Star

Sign of the Rainbow

Sign of the Sun

Sign of the World

Junior Girl Scout Signs

Junior Girl Scouts may also earn four awards called signs, each one based on one of the four program goals of Girl Scouting. They are the Sign of the Star, the Sign of the Rainbow, the Sign of the Sun, and the Sign of the World. Details on how to earn the signs can be found in the *Junior Girl Scout Handbook.*

Religious Awards

Junior Girl Scouts may earn a variety of religious awards. Use the following chart to contact the organizations that can help girls earn specific awards.

Religious Organization	Award	Where To Get Information
African Methodist Episcopal (A.M.E.)	Grades 4 & 5 God and Family	P.R.A.Y. 8520 Mackenzie Rd, Ste. 3 St. Louis, MO 63123-3413 (800) 933-7729
Baha'i	Unity of Mankind	Baha'i National Center, Education and Schools Office 1233 Central St Evanston, IL 60201 (847) 869-9039
Buddhist	Ages 6-8 Padma Award	Buddhist National Committee on Scouting 701 E. Thrift Ave Kingsland, GA 31548-8213 (912) 729-6323
Christian Church (Disciples of Christ)	Grades 4 & 5 God and Family	P.R.A.Y. 8520 Mackenzie Rd, Ste. 3 St. Louis, MO 63123-3413 (800) 933-7729
Christian Science	Ages 9 & 10 Christian Science God and Country	P.R.A.Y. 8520 Mackenzie Rd, Ste. 3 St. Louis, MO 63123-3413 (800) 933-7729
Churches of Christ	Grades 4 & 5 Joyful Servant Award Grades 6-8 Good Servant Award	Members of Churches of Christ for Scouting ACU Box 27938 Abilene, TX 79699-7938 (915) 674-3739
Eastern Orthodox	Ages 9 & 10 Chi-Rho	P.R.A.Y. 8520 Mackenzie Rd, Ste. 3 St. Louis, MO 63123-3413 (800) 933-7729
Episcopal	Grades 4 & 5 God and Family	P.R.A.Y. 8520 Mackenzie Rd, Ste. 3 St. Louis, MO 63123-3413 (800) 933-7729
Hindu	Ages 8-11 Grades 3-6 Dharma Award	North American Hindu Association 847 E. Angela Pleasanton, CA 94566 (925) 846-3811
Islamic	Ages 9-11 In the Name of Allah Award	Islamic Committee on Girl Scouting 31 Marian St Stamford, CT 06907 (203) 359-3593
Jewish	Ages 9-11 Bat Or Award	National Jewish Girl Scout Committee 33 Central Dr. Bronxville, NY 10708-4603 (914) 738-3986 or (718) 252-6072

Lutheran	Grades 4 & 5 God and Family	P.R.A.Y. 8520 Mackenzie Rd, Ste. 3 St. Louis, MO 63123-3413 (800) 933-7729
Church of Christ of Latter-Day Saints (Mormon)	Ages 10 & 11 Gospel in Action Award	Salt Lake District Center Church of Jesus Christ of Latter-day Saints, Young Women's Department 76 N. Main St Salt Lake City, UT 84150 (801) 240-2141
Polish National Catholic Church	God and Community Award	National Committee on Scouting Polish National Catholic Church 115 Heather Hill Dr Buffalo, NY 14224
Presbyterian Church U.S.A.	Grades 4 & 5 God and Family	P.R.A.Y. 8520 Mackenzie Rd, Ste. 3 St. Louis, MO 63123-3413 (800) 933-7729
Protestant and Independent Christian Churches	Grades 4 & 5 God and Family	P.R.A.Y. 8520 Mackenzie Rd, Ste. 3 St. Louis, MO 63123-3413 (800) 933-7729
Religious Society of Friends (Quakers)	Grades 4 & 5 That of God	P.R.A.Y. 8520 Mackenzie Rd, Ste. 3 St. Louis, MO 63123-3413 (800) 933-7729
Reorganized Church of Jesus Christ of Latter-Day Saints	Ages 9 & 10 Light of the World Age 11 Liahona	Youth Ministries Office The Auditorium PO Box 1059 Independence, MO 64051 (816) 833-1000 Ext 1374
Roman Catholic Church	Ages 9-11 I Live My Faith	National Federation for Catholic Youth Ministry 415 Michigan Ave Washington DC 20017-1518 (202) 636-3825
Unitarian Universalist	Ages 9-11 Religion in Life	Unitarian Universalist Association ATTN: Bookstore 25 Beacon St Boston, MA 02108 (617) 742-2100 Ext 102 or (800) 215-9076
United Church of Christ	Grades 4 & 5 God and Family	P.R.A.Y. 8520 Mackenzie Rd, Ste. 3 St. Louis, MO 63123-3413 (800) 933-7729
United Methodist	Grades 4 & 5 God and Family	P.R.A.Y. 8520 Mackenzie Rd, Ste. 3 St. Louis, MO 63123-3413 (800) 933-7729
Unity Church	Ages 9-11 God in Me	Association of Unity Churches PO Box 610 Lee's Summit, MO 64063 (816) 524-7414

Junior Girl Scout Uniform

Wearing a uniform is one way of showing you belong to an organization. No one—girls or adults—are required to own a uniform or a specific number of pieces; however, many leaders and girls enjoy wearing their uniforms for special events, meetings, and ceremonies. Your Girl Scout council may offer assistance in supplying uniforms to those unable to afford them. Check with your local council representative.

Adult Uniform

Junior Girl Scout Insignia

If you want to learn more about Girl Scout insignia, look at the insignia chart on the "Just for Girls" pages of the Girl Scout Web site *www.girlscouts.org/girls*.

The insignia chart shows at a glance the age levels at which girls can earn various awards and participation patches. Also included in the chart is a list of emblems that relate to membership in the Girl Scout organization.

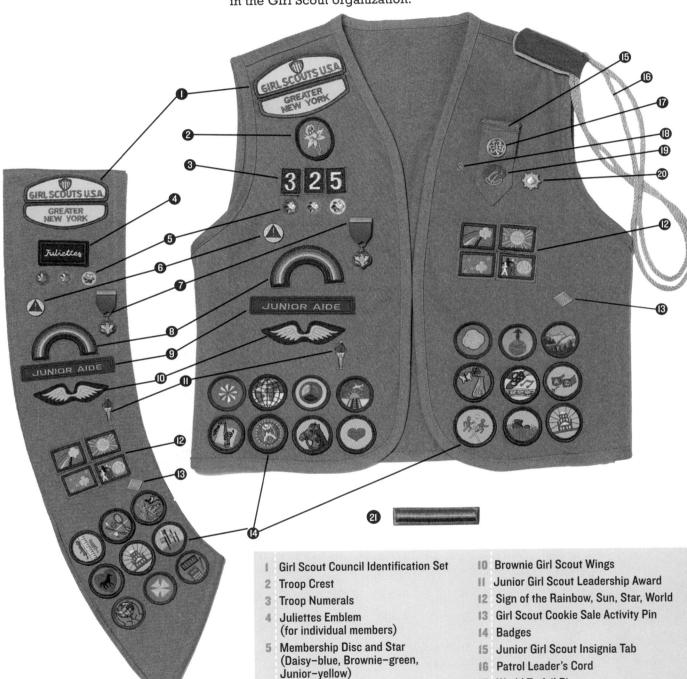

1 Girl Scout Council Identification Set	10 Brownie Girl Scout Wings
2 Troop Crest	11 Junior Girl Scout Leadership Award
3 Troop Numerals	12 Sign of the Rainbow, Sun, Star, World
4 Juliettes Emblem (for individual members)	13 Girl Scout Cookie Sale Activity Pin
5 Membership Disc and Star (Daisy–blue, Brownie–green, Junior–yellow)	14 Badges
	15 Junior Girl Scout Insignia Tab
	16 Patrol Leader's Cord
6 Safety Award	17 World Trefoil Pin
7 Medal of Honor Lifesaving Award	18 Membership Numeral Guard
8 Bridge to Junior Girl Scouts	19 Girl Scout Membership Pin
9 Junior Aide Award	20 Girl Scout Bronze Award
	21 Bridge to Cadette Girl Scouts

Adult Insignia

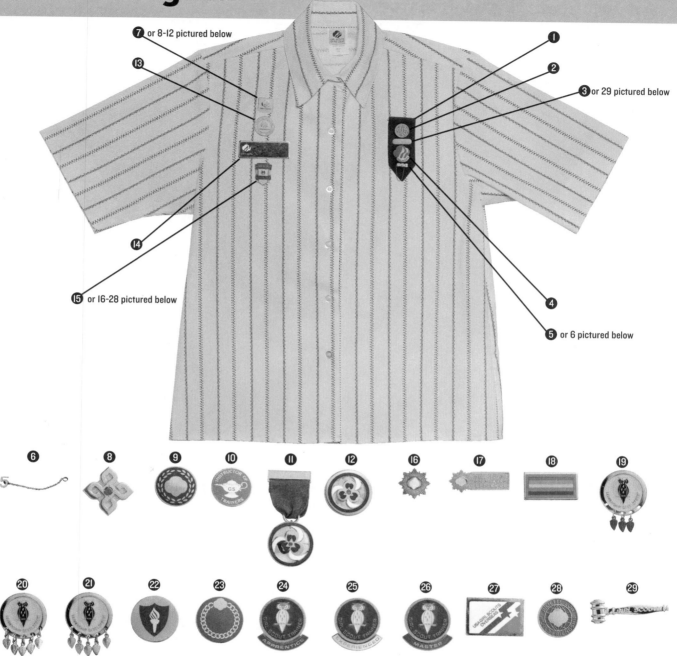

1	Adult Insignia Tab	11	Thanks Badge
2	World Trefoil Pin	12	Thanks Badge II
3	Adult Position Pin	13	Lifetime Membership Pin
4	Girl Scout Membership Pin	14	Personalized ID Pin
5	Campus Girl Scout Guard	15	Years of Service Pin
6	Membership Numeral Guard	16	Miniature of Gold Award/Parent Pin*
7	Appreciation Pin	17	Girl Scout Gold Alliance
8	Certified Executive Directors Pin	18	Bridge to Adult Girl Scout
9	Honor Pin	19	Leadership Development Pin, Green
10	Instructor-of-Trainers Pin	20	Leadership Development Pin, Silver

21	Leadership Development Pin, Gold
22	Outstanding Leader Award
23	Outstanding Volunteer Pin
24	Trainer's Pin, Apprentice
25	Trainer's Pin, Experienced
26	Trainer's Pin, Master
27	USA Girl Scouts Overseas Pin
28	Juliette Low World Friendship Pin
29	Outgoing President's Pin

Note: To avoid a cluttered appearance, only a few pins and awards should be worn at one time. If an adult has received more than one special recognition (e.g., Appreciation Pin, Honor Pin), the last one received is generally the one worn on the uniform.

*May be worn by significant adult(s) associated with a girl's earning the Girl Scout Gold Award.

Bridging Ceremony

Bridging ceremonies mark a girl's moving up to the next membership level. For more information about bridging ceremonies, see the ceremony section and worksheet in the *Junior Girl Scout Handbook*.

The bridge that takes Girl Scouts into the next program level may be represented in many ways. The bridge can be a natural or a homemade bridge that girls walk over. It can be an arch that girls walk under, steps they ascend and descend, or stepping stones (real or constructed) that they walk over. The bridge can even be represented by a walk from one side of the room to the other.

Often, as in the sample ceremony at right, the Junior Girl Scout troop stands on one side of the bridge, and the Cadette Girl Scout troop on the other side. Each Junior Girl Scout is met halfway by a Cadette Girl Scout from the troop she is entering.

Bridge to Cadette Girl Scouts

Supplies: Decorations, bridge construction materials, and a flower for each bridging Junior Girl Scout.

Procedure: Each Cadette Girl Scout will present her Junior Girl Scout partner with a challenge taken from the Girl Scout Law. Junior Girl Scouts will respond to the challenge by stating how they will meet it. Some time for rehearsals is helpful.

Sample Script

Bridging Ceremony

Junior Girl Scout Leader: _____(names of girls) have fulfilled their responsibilities as Junior Girl Scouts. They have served their community, their troop, and the Girl Scout movement well, and are prepared to bridge into Cadette Girl Scouts. Today we are locking in our hearts the fun, laughter, hard work, and good times that their Junior Girl Scout years have brought.

Speaker #2: As each girl's name is called, she will walk across the bridge to Cadette Girl Scouts. One of her Cadette Girl Scout sisters will meet her halfway.

Leader: _____(Junior GS #1's name) walks to the middle of the bridge and is met by _____(Cadette GS #1's name).

Cadette #1: _____(Junior #1's name), I challenge you to do your best to be honest and fair.

(Cadette #1 hands Junior #1 a flower.)

Junior #1: I will be honest and fair by _____(the girl's own words). *(Then both girls walk together to stand with the other Cadette Girl Scouts. Each girl is met in the same fashion. Each challenge spoken by a Cadette Girl Scout is one part of the Girl Scout Law. All 10 parts of the Law are stated. Parts could be repeated for more than 10 girls, or girls could be given more parts if there are fewer than 10 girls.)*

Leader: _____(Junior GS #2's name) walks to the middle of the bridge and is met by _____(Cadette GS #2's name).

Cadette #2: _____(Junior #2's name), I challenge you to do your best to be friendly and helpful.

Junior #2: I will be friendly and helpful by _____ (the girl's own words).

Cadette #3: _____(Junior #3's name), I challenge you to be considerate and caring.

Junior #3: I will be considerate and caring by _____ (the girl's own words).

And so on through the 10 parts of the Girl Scout Law.
Cadette Girl Scout Leader: *(after all the girls have crossed over)* Cadette Girl Scout troop # ___ welcomes their new sisters and looks forward to the fun and adventure to come.

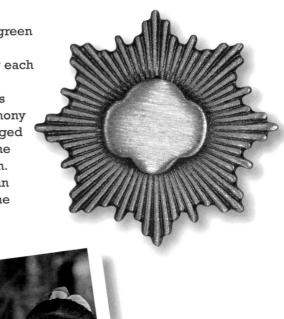

The Girl Scout Bronze Award is the highest award for Junior Girl Scouts. This sample ceremony gives each girl the opportunity to describe her project and to identify what she learned in the process.

Supplies: Three tall white or green candles. These candles are surrounded by one candle for each girl receiving her Girl Scout Bronze Award. The tall candles should be lit before the ceremony begins. Candles can be arranged in a candle log on a table at the head of a horseshoe formation.

Procedure: This ceremony can begin with a flag ceremony, the pledge of allegiance, the Girl Scout Promise, and a song.

Sample Script

Bronze Award Ceremony

Leader: Today we are honoring _____(names of girls to receive award) for earning the highest award in Junior Girl Scouting, the Girl Scout Bronze Award. Each of these girls has achieved the high ideals and goals expressed by Juliette Gordon Low, who founded the Girl Scout movement in 1912.

Speaker #2: The three tall candles symbolize the threefold purpose of Girl Scouting as expressed in our Promise.

Speaker #3: "On my honor, I will try: To serve God and my country..."

Speaker #4: "...To help people at all times..."

Speaker #5: "...And to live by the Girl Scout Law."

Leader: _____(names of girls) have served their country, community, and God with their hard work and skills. Each will speak about her Girl Scout Bronze Award project and receive her award. *(Call the first girl by name).*

Award Recipient #1: *(Stepping forward)* My Girl Scout Bronze Award project was _____. I learned _____.

(She walks to the leader who gives her the Girl Scout Bronze Award. Then she goes to the table, picks up a candle, lights it from one of the tall candles, and puts it back down.)

Leader: _____*(Calls the next girl by name).*

Award Recipient #2: *(Stepping forward)* My Girl Scout Bronze Award project was _____. I learned _____.

(She walks to the leader who gives her the Girl Scout Bronze Award. Then she goes to the table, picks up a candle, lights it from one of the tall candles, and puts it back down. This continues until each girl has spoken, received her award, and lit her candle.)

Leader: An award is a symbol of achievement. It means that you have learned something and provided service to others. With each new award, a Girl Scout takes on new responsibilities. More is expected at home, in Girl Scouting, and in your community. Strive always to be worthy of the symbols you wear, and wear them with pride. Best wishes to each of you!

Closing: *Retire colors, sing a song of your choice, form a friendship circle.*

A Girl Scout's Own Ceremony

This ceremony honors Juliette Gordon Low's global vision of world unity and friendship through the Girl Scout movement. Each girl should prepare her own statement on how she feels about world friendship, or what she believes her role is in creating a world where people live in friendship and cooperation. The spoken parts in this ceremony are examples for those who need help.

Theme: World Friendship

Objective: For each Girl Scout to add her link of special feelings, thoughts, and talents to create a World Friendship Chain

Supplies: Strips of color construction paper (orange, red, yellow, purple, brown, pink) of equal length for each girl. Each strip should have a piece of tape at one end. These strips will create a friendship chain. A larger green link representing the Girl Scout movement should already be formed.

Procedure: The ceremony begins with the leader holding the green link in her hands. She makes her statement and adds her link to the large green link. She then passes the beginnings of the chain to the first girl, who makes her statement and adds her link to the leader's link. Either the first girl or the leader can hold the chain as each girl adds her link to the one that was added before her. After the final girl has added her link, the leader makes a statement, and then attaches the last link to the large green link. This forms a complete circle.

Sample Script

A Girl Scout's Own Ceremony

Leader: *(Holding the large green circle up for all to see)* Long ago, Juliette Gordon Low had a vision. She saw girls from all over the world breaking out of traditional roles to develop their true potential. She saw girls working together, helping each other, and uniting in friendship. Juliette Low founded the Girl Scout movement in the United States and turned it into an international movement. Through Girl Scouts and Girl Guides, girls and women from cultures all over the world are linked together. *(The leader lifts up her link)* I bring to the Girl Scout movement my ability to help girls live by the Girl Scout Promise and Law. I am a special link in the chain of Girl Scouting. *(The leader tapes her link to the large green link, and passes it to Girl #1.)*

Girl #1: I bring to the Girl Scout movement my ability to _____ (play the piano/be kind and considerate/help young children learn to read). I am a special link in the chain of Girl Scouting.

(She tapes her link to the leader's link, then passes it to Girl #2, and the ceremony continues in this manner.)

Girl #2: I bring to the Girl Scout movement my ability to _____ (use the computer/play soccer/make friends easily). I am a special link in the chain of Girl Scouting.

Girl #3: I bring to the Girl Scout movement my ability to _____ (make lasagna/organize an activity/be loyal). I am a special link in the chain of Girl Scouting.

Girl #4: I bring to the Girl Scout movement my ability to _____ (have fun/respect myself and others/figure out math problems). I am a special link in the chain of Girl Scouting.

Closing: When the final girl has attached her link to the chain, she hands it to the leader. The leader attaches the final link to the large green Girl Scout link.

Leader: When we link our special talents together, we create a strong Girl Scout movement. We connect with our sisters around the world to bring peace, respect, and joy into the world.

The ceremony can end with a song.

Junior Girl Scouts and Money

Managing Troop or Group Money

Junior Girl Scouts can understand budgeting and group finances. They are capable of deciding whether to spend all their money on a party, to use it toward a service project, or to save it for future plans. Experiences in Girl Scouting can help girls learn to manage money wisely.

Your troop or group should have a checking account with a council identification number. Check with your Girl Scout council for specific information on policies for troop or group checking accounts. All girls should be aware of the amount of money in the treasury and how funds are expended. If your community does not have a bank in a convenient location, contact your council for assistance in investigating banking by mail.

Girls should understand that the money in the treasury is not theirs or yours, but rather belongs to the troop as it functions within the greater context of Girl Scouting. Any money given or earned to support the troop is to be used by girls to support program activities. The same is true of any equipment or supplies acquired by your troop or group.

Keep accurate records of income and expenses, and save written invoices and sales slips. You should never mix your personal funds with Girl Scout money. If you use money from the treasury to buy supplies, be sure to show it as an expense and have receipts. If you add your own money, record that as income.

Troop dues are the amount of money the girls in your troop have decided each will add to the troop treasury. Keep in mind, however, that participation in Girl Scouting does not depend on, nor are girls required to pay, troop or group dues. Money-earning activities may be planned and carried out by girls supported by adults to supplement the funds in the treasury. Such items as Girl Scout cookies and calendars can be sold as part of council-sponsored product sales in which troops participate. *Safety-Wise* outlines broad standards and guidelines for council-sponsored sales. For example:

- Permission must be obtained in writing from a girl's parent or guardian before she participates in money-earning activities or council-sponsored product sales.

- Each girl's participation should be voluntary, and the number of money-earning projects should not exceed what is needed to support troop activities.

- Girl Scouts, in their Girl Scout capacities, may not solicit money for other organizations.

Reminder

Before starting money-earning activities, read the relevant pages in *Safety-Wise*, obtain written permission from your Girl Scout council, and check with your Girl Scout council regarding any pertinent laws, regulations, or insurance requirements.

Girls need to play an active role in planning and carrying out all money-earning activities. Selling products, such as cookies and calendars should enhance a girl's experience in Girl Scouting. Money-earning activities are part of the Girl Scout program and should be designed to increase decision-making, planning, and goal-setting skills. Chapter 2 of the *Junior Girl Scout Handbook*, "Adventures in Girl Scouting," contains information on cookie sales and money-earning activities.

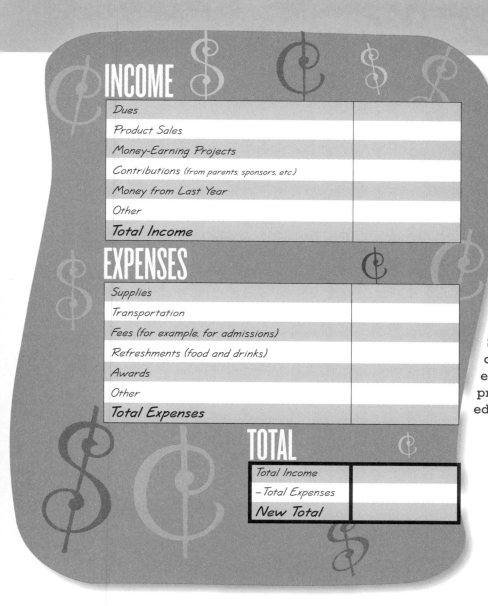

INCOME

Dues	
Product Sales	
Money-Earning Projects	
Contributions (from parents, sponsors, etc.)	
Money from Last Year	
Other	
Total Income	

EXPENSES

Supplies	
Transportation	
Fees (for example, for admissions)	
Refreshments (food and drinks)	
Awards	
Other	
Total Expenses	

TOTAL

Total Income	
– Total Expenses	
New Total	

Making Money Decisions with Girls

Try to ensure that decisions about raising and spending money reflect the needs and interests of all the girls in your troop/group. When planning trips and activities with girls, remind them to consider everyone's opinion and develop a plan agreeable to everyone. Girls don't join Girl Scouts to sell things. Spending an inordinate amount of time on raising money for one expensive trip or event can prevent girls from having other educational and fun experiences.

What if?

What happens to the money if your troop or group disbands? In some cases, leaders and girls plan a large party as a way to use up all of the money in the treasury.

But, what message does this send to the girls? What they are learning is "this is our money and we don't want anyone else to get it."

If, from the beginning, girls have not thought of the money in their troop treasury as belonging to them individually, but as money given to them on behalf of Girl Scouting, then other uses for this money become more appropriate. Girls can:

• Brainstorm a list of equipment to purchase and donate to their council for other Girl Scouts to enjoy.

• Use the money to benefit a council camp or a program center.

• Decide to donate the money to a community project or other cause.

Selling Girl Scout Cookies

The cookie sale has long been an important program activity in Girl Scouting. In 1923, in an issue of *American Girl* (a magazine once produced by Girl Scouts of the USA), Girl Scouts from Bridgeport, Connecticut, discussed how they baked and sold cookies to fund troop activities. By 1936, Girl Scout councils had their first nationally franchised Girl Scout cookie sale. At the end of World War II, the Girl Scout cookie sale became more visible as interest in Girl Scout camps grew and profits helped girls everywhere enjoy the benefits of the Girl Scout camp experience.

You play an essential role in helping girls learn all the valuable skills that are part of participating in the Girl Scout cookie sale. The experience girls get in setting goals and the opportunity to see firsthand how individual and group efforts contribute to reaching goals can provide lifelong lessons.

For many girls, this may be their first real experience in essential money management skills—budgeting, accounting, investing, and allocating funds. Girls also practice important interpersonal skills as they learn how to relate to different people in different ways.

Involve girls in all aspects of the sale. Make sure they are part of all the decision-making. This will ensure that success at the end will be theirs.

Girls can earn the "Cookie Connection" badge by completing the activities described in the *Junior Girl Scout Badge Book*. Each year, girls can earn the Girl Scout Cookie Sale Activity Pin. Pamphlets that describe activities girls must do to earn a particular year's Girl Scout Cookie Sale Activity Pin are available from your council or NES.

▶ Internet Sales Policy

The policy on Internet sales adopted by Girl Scouts of the USA's National Board of Directors states: Sales on the Internet of any products sold in "council-sponsored product sales," such as Girl Scout cookies, candy, nuts, calendars, or magazine subscriptions, may not be conducted by anyone at any time. Sales on the Internet include on-line auctions, broadcast e-mail messages, and/or posting on individual Girl Scout, troop/group, or Girl Scout council Web sites.

Where the Money Goes

Today's cookie sale profits still build and maintain Girl Scout camps, but they do so much more—train and support leaders, underwrite the costs of special activities, finance travel scholarships, and make Girl Scouting accessible to all girls, including girls in places like homeless shelters and migrant camps. Cookie sales also help the Girl Scout council office recruit and organize troops or groups, train Girl Scout leaders, and operate council-sponsored program activities (including special workshops for leaders, day trips, and award ceremonies). The annual Girl Scout cookie sale helps ensure that the Girl Scout program can continue to meet the needs and interests of every girl everywhere.

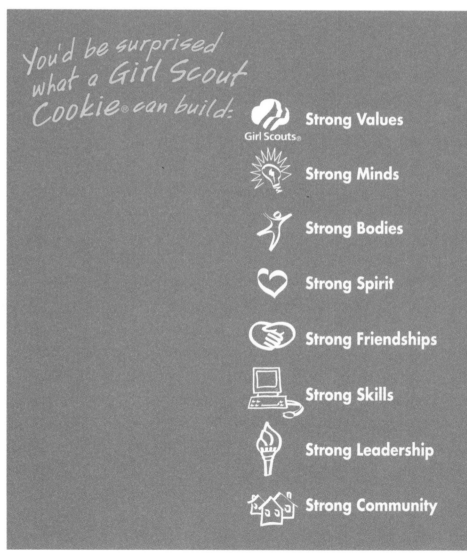

You'd be surprised what a Girl Scout Cookie® can build:

Girl Scouts® Strong Values

Strong Minds

Strong Bodies

Strong Spirit

Strong Friendships

Strong Skills

Strong Leadership

Strong Community

Important Places and Faces

Use this section to keep a record of important phone numbers and addresses so you can have them at your fingertips.

IMPORTANT INFORMATION

Council name: _____

Address : _____

_____

Phone number: _____

Name of council contact: _____

Phone number at troop meeting site: _____

Camp address: _____

_____

Local police department number: _____

Poison control number: _____

She Told a Friend and She Told a Friend and So On

Sometimes plans change and you need to get in touch with the parents or guardians of the girls in your troop or group in a hurry. Create a phone chain to help expedite this process. You call the first person on the list and then each adult is responsible for making one or two calls. This will save you the time and energy that it takes to contact every member of your troop.

name: _____

telephone: _____

e-mail: _____

name: _____

telephone: _____

e-mail: _____

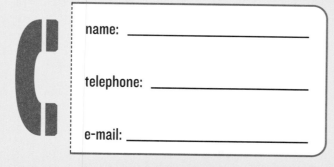

name: _____

telephone: _____

e-mail: _____

name: _____

telephone: _____

e-mail: _____

name: _____

telephone: _____

e-mail: _____

name: _____

telephone: _____

e-mail: _____

name: _____

telephone: _____

e-mail: _____

name: _____

telephone: _____

e-mail: _____

Junior Girl Scout Resources

The basic components of the Girl Scout program for 8-11 year olds can be found in two primary publications, the *Junior Girl Scout Handbook* and the *Junior Girl Scout Badge Book*. Together, these books offer a wide variety of information and activities that will meet the needs and interests of the girls in your troop or group.

Junior Girl Scout Handbook

The *Junior Girl Scout Handbook* has 10 chapters and contains topics ranging from planning trips to tying knots to exploring technology. Girls are not expected to read their handbooks like a novel, from page one to the end. Instead, they may jump from topic to topic or page to page. As girls develop new interests and skills, the handbook offers basic information that will inspire them to dig deeper and explore further, using badges, service projects, the Girl Scout Bronze Award, or other Girl Scout activities they choose to do.

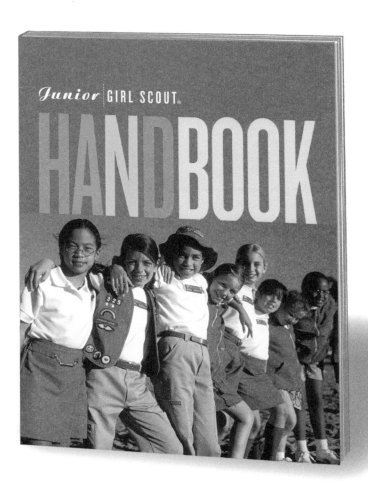

Junior Girl Scout Badge Book

Earning awards is one aspect of Girl Scouting that makes it unique among youth serving organizations. Junior Girl Scouts will work on earning the awards found in the *Junior Girl Scout Badge Book*. With more than 100 badges to choose from, girls should be able to sharpen skills they have already acquired while exploring new interests. Girls should be encouraged to dabble in areas that are entirely unfamiliar to them. However, if a girl begins a badge and decides that she is not interested in its activities, she can stop and try something else.

Often, girls this age enjoy working together in groups. Girls in a troop or group are not only allowed to work together to earn awards, but they are also encouraged to do so. If several girls (or even a whole troop) do a badge together, girls will have an opportunity to explore the topic more thoroughly. In addition, you will not have to divide your time and attention among multiple needs, resources, or consultants.

Finally, the chapters in the *Junior Girl Scout Badge Book* correspond to the *Junior Girl Scout Handbook*. In other words, the same chapters appear in both books in the same order. This means that if girls like the handbook chapter on family and friends, for example, they can go to the same chapter in the badge book to find out what awards they can earn on that topic. Also, both books contain a metric conversion chart. Activities in both books that include measurements are footnoted so that you and the girls can find metric equivalents on the charts.

2 The Key to Successful Planning

Girl/Adult Partnership

A key to successful planning with Junior Girl Scouts is to forge a girl/adult partnership. When girls are active planners and decision-makers, their competence and self-esteem grow. Research conducted by Girl Scouts of the USA has found that Junior Girl Scouts who are encouraged to take the lead and be involved in troop decision-making are more likely to enjoy their Girl Scout program activities and stay with them longer.

Start building a strong partnership with your Junior Girl Scouts as soon as you meet them. Active listening helps create an atmosphere where girl/adult partnership and planning can thrive. Listening to your girls' concerns in a non-judgmental way will encourage them to do most of the talking. In some cases, as the adult, you will have to make some final decisions, especially where safety is a concern. Some girls may have more experience in a particular activity than you do. In that case, they should take the lead in planning it. For instance, a girl who is an accomplished hiker could help plot a trail or plan an outdoor adventure.

Troop or Group Government

Girl Scouting has a built-in structure to help leaders sustain their girl/adult planning and efforts. This structure is traditionally referred to as troop or group government. There are three models: the patrol system, the executive board (also called the steering committee), and the town meeting. In the patrol system and the executive board system, some girls represent others in special meetings, though each girl gets to vote on all important troop matters.

Three Models of Troop Government

	Patrol	*Executive Board*	*Town Meeting*
HOW IT IS ORGANIZED	The troop divides into small groups called patrols. (Good for medium to large troops)	One leadership team is elected to represent the entire troop. (Good for smaller troops)	The troop has no formal government. The entire troop participates directly in the decision-making process.
HOW IT WORKS	Patrols choose patrol name, patrol symbol, patrol leaders, and assistant patrol leaders. A kaper chart lists jobs and who does them.	The troop elects girls to the leadership team, which sometimes is called the steering committee. The team then elects its officers (President, Secretary, Treasurer). The number of officers varies with the projects.	Troop business is discussed and determined by all girls in the troop. This system requires a moderator. The moderator guides troop discussion.
HOW LONG IT LASTS	Members of the patrol should rotate the leadership jobs so that everyone has an opportunity.	The length of time in leadership positions should be limited to give each girl an opportunity to lead.	Rotate the moderator position so everyone gets a chance to lead.

The Patrol System

In the patrol system, the troop or group divides into small groups, with every member playing a role. Patrols of four to six girls are recommended so that each girl gets a chance to participate and express her opinions.

Patrols may be organized by interests or by tasks—performing activities that feed into a project. Each patrol takes responsibility for some part of the total project. For example, one patrol can be responsible for setup, another for clean-up.

The Executive Board

In the executive board system (also called steering committee), there is one leadership team for the whole troop or group called an executive board. This system often works well with smaller troops and groups. The board's main responsibility is to help make plans and assign jobs based on interests and needs.

The executive board usually has a president, a vice president, a secretary, and a treasurer, and holds its own meetings to discuss troop or group matters. The number of officers can vary. The length of time each girl serves on the executive board should be limited so that all troop or group members can participate during the year. The girls decide how to pass their ideas and suggestions to the executive board throughout the year.

The Town Meeting

Under the town meeting system, business is discussed and decisions are made at meetings attended by all the girls. As in the two other systems, everyone gets the chance to participate in decision-making and leadership. This system usually requires a moderator who makes sure that everyone gets a chance to talk and that all ideas are considered.

In any governing system, rules can be adapted to fit the situation. Health and safety rules, however, must be strictly adhered to at all times. Keep *Safety-Wise* on hand to refer to regularly.

Planning Activities with Junior Girl Scouts

Activities found in the Girl Scout resources vary in the time it takes to complete them, the materials needed, and their level of complexity. This variety ensures that all Junior Girl Scouts can find activities they will enjoy.

There are so many choices in Girl Scouting. Help girls explore activities in other resources—beyond the *Junior Girl Scout Handbook* and *Junior Girl Scout Badge Book*, including: *Issues for Girl Scouts* booklets, *Games for Girl Scouts, Outdoor Education in Girl Scouting, Octavia's Girl Scout Journey*, and *Strength in Sharing: Philanthropy in Girl Scouting*. A complete resource list is at the end of this book.

Encourage girls to sample activities they have not tried before. Help them understand what an activity entails and what can be accomplished realistically.

Planning Tips

The following tips will help you manage activities:

• Agree on what you will do and what the girls will do.

• Decide whether you need help from other adults or your Girl Scout council.

• Evaluate why you and the girls are doing this particular activity.

• Simplify a project or develop a time line when needed.

• Show girls how to make the project more exciting, inclusive, and accessible. Consider if the activity needs to be adapted to ensure access for all girls.

• Break activities into steps. Allow time for planning and gathering resources.

• Make a chart to display tasks or steps in the activity.

• Consider cost, permission slips, transportation, supplies or equipment, and other practical matters.

• Remember that abilities and development among Junior Girl Scouts vary significantly. For example, some girls may be more advanced in physical coordination skills while others may have better writing skills.

• Help girls handle frustration when it surfaces. Show them how to change plans, if needed. Know when to suggest they take a break or simply take a different approach. Keep the fun optimal and stress minimal.

• Be prepared for everything and anything! Be creative. Always have something ready to do, such as a song or quick game, if the planned activities finish early.

Multi-Age Troops and Groups

Girl Scout troops and groups might include girls of different ages and from different grade levels. In multi-age groups, younger girls can learn social, physical, and intellectual skills from older girls. Older girls, acting as role models, strengthen their self-confidence and skills by sharing their expertise with younger girls. When older girls are paired with younger girls, leaders benefit by being given some time to focus on an individual girl or situation.

Make sure your Junior Girl Scout patrols contain a mix of ages. In the beginning of the year, it may be appropriate for older girls to assume leadership positions. As the year progresses, make sure younger girls are provided with the opportunity to fill those positions.

► **Older girls can model the duties and responsibilities of troop or group government for younger girls.**

Emphasize to girls the positive aspects of a multi-age level troop or group so that everyone feels welcome. Do not divide girls strictly into older and younger groupings. Encourage girls to look actively for opportunities to assist one another.

Adapting Troop or Group Activities

Each Girl Scout troop or group tailors the Girl Scout program to its own interests, abilities, and resources. Here are some ways to adapt activities:

- Change the method. For example, if an onsite visit is not possible, see a relevant film or have a speaker come to a meeting.

- Modify the activity. If you are visiting a museum to view sculpture, for example, find out if a girl who is blind might be given permission to touch the pieces.

- Substitute an activity that meets the same purpose. If part of an obstacle course or relay race requires girls to run, girls who are unable to run could be asked to walk, or do another type of physical activity.

If adaptation is not possible, a decision can be made not to do the activity at all. Similarly, if an activity violates the religious tradition of a girl, it should not be done. The needs and feelings of girls always come first.

Planning Troop Meetings

In general, Junior Girl Scout troop or group meetings last 60-90 minutes and take place once a week or twice a month. The length and frequency of meetings depend on the needs and interests of the girls. Some Junior Girl Scout troops or groups meet once a month for three hours. When engaged in a project, a troop or group may meet twice a week for two months.

What should you do? Ask the girls! Consider everyone's availability, including your own, and base your decision about meetings on the projects, ideas, and plans that the girls have.

The following is one model for a meeting. This design should be discussed with the girls and modified, if necessary. Flexibility on your part is highly encouraged.

1. Start-Up Activity

The start-up activity can be something girls do alone or in pairs as they arrive. The activity should not require a great deal of time to complete or clean up, and should allow you time to greet each girl individually and talk to her parents if necessary. Possible activities are:

- **A simple game:** Have materials available for girls to create their own games or for girls to teach each other a new game. You might suggest that they learn some of the games from *Games for Girl Scouts*. See "Egg Carton and Ball Game" on the next page, which is one game from this book.

- **A group poster or mural:** Invite girls to design a poster or mural based on a theme of interest.

- **Journal writing:** Ask girls to record anything interesting that has happened to them since the last meeting. Or, they can write about a problem they are experiencing. Allow a few minutes for girls to share their thoughts with others.

- **New Girl Scout resources:** Encourage girls to try some of the activities in a new Girl Scout resource.

- **Read magazines or books:** Check with your local school or library to see if they will donate used books. Girls can use these for relaxation or for ideas or inspiration to write poems, stories, or a group song.

2. Opening

The opening is the first activity that the girls do as a group. It provides focus and structure. Girls should take turns planning the opening activity. Possibilities for the opening:

- Conduct a flag ceremony.

- Ask each girl to share something exciting that has happened in school or with her family or friends.

- Sing a song or recite a poem.

- Ask each girl to share one way she utilized a part of the Girl Scout Promise or Law since the last meeting.

3. Business

Troop or group business could include making special announcements, taking attendance, collecting troop dues or fees, planning for trips or activities, or revising the current kaper chart. Involve girls in conducting this part of the meeting.

4. Activities

Activities can be done alone, in pairs, or as a group. Choice of activities should be girl-directed and can cover a range of interests. See "Evaluating Troop or Group Activities" in Section 5 to assess the overall effectiveness of activities.

In addition to the *Junior Girl Scout Handbook* and *Junior Girl Scout Badge Book*, there are many other resources full of activities appropriate for Junior Girl Scouts. See the list at the end of this book.

Activity:

Egg Carton and Ball Game

What You Need
- An egg carton
- A table tennis ball
- Scissors
- Markers

What You Do

1. To prepare the egg carton, cut the lid off the egg carton. Number each compartment consecutively.

2. To play, each girl holds the egg carton in front of her body. She places the Ping-Pong ball in the #1 compartment. She must toss the ball in the air and attempt to catch it in the #2 compartment. Count the number of attempts that it takes to move the ball through the six or 12 compartments.

Variation: With two players, have the girls face each other about three feet apart. Each must toss the ball to her partner five times. Each time it lands in a compartment, the number is noted. Add the numbers of each of the five tosses. The girl with the highest score wins.

5. Cleanup

Use the kaper chart to assign clean-up responsibility, rotating duties among all members of your troop or group. Never use clean-up as a disciplinary tool. Clean-up should be viewed as a necessary component of a successful meeting, not as punishment.

6. Closing

The closing should focus on what the girls accomplished and what they can expect at the next meeting. Suggestions for closing activities:

- Sing a song or recite a poem.

- Say the Girl Scout Promise.

- Discuss the meaning of one part of the Girl Scout Law.

- Gather for the friendship circle.

- Ask girls to state individual goals they would like to accomplish.

- Highlight something for the girls to look forward to at the next meeting.

It is necessary to be aware of each girl's arrangements for getting home. After the closing, be sure each girl is met by her parent, guardian, or other adult.

Make a Meeting Plan Worksheet

Design your own planning worksheets to keep in your notebook or folder. During the year, read through the planning sheets to review plans and goals. Determine what was accomplished and what still needs to be done. You may want to draw a planning sheet on paper, poster board, or on the computer. Here are some sample topics for your worksheet:

- What we will do and the length of time it will take

- Who will do it

- Materials and resources

- Additional notes for follow-up

3 Beyond Badges

You and the girls in your troop or group may want to go beyond those activities found in the basic Junior Girl Scout resources. Expand their opportunities by looking at the ideas on the following pages.

Girl Scout Basics

Trips

Find out more about how signs, logos, badges, and uniforms are made. Visit:

- A local printer/engraver's shop

- A design studio or clothing manufacturer

- A store that sells embroidery items

Girl Scouts refer to the Promise and the Law to set a code of conduct. How are laws made in other organizations and in government? Get an appointment to tour or visit:

- The state legislature when in session

- The United Nations

- A Congressional representative, mayor, or other official

- A civil court where citizens serve on juries

Activities

Learn more about the Girl Scout uniform by designing Girl Scout paper dolls and uniform components from different eras. Share some facts and tales about each uniform with younger Girl Scouts. What do clothes in different eras tell you about women's lives? Contact the Girl Scout Historic Preservation office at GSUSA, the Juliette Gordon Low Center in Savannah, or your council staff for more information about the history of Girl Scout uniforms and badges.

Discussion Topics

Discuss aspects of the Girl Scout Promise and Law. Pose questions for reflection, such as:

- What does respecting authority mean to you? When, if ever, is it okay not to respect authority? Give examples to support your position.

- How can you be a sister to every Girl Scout? What are three ways you will try to be a better sister to every Girl Scout in the next week?

- What does courage mean to you? How can you be more courageous?

You may want to pose a discussion question for each part of the Promise and Law. Assign a topic to think about over the week and then discuss it when you next meet.

Service Projects

Share your successes at council-wide or multi-council events or training sessions. Create swaps that are distinctly representative of your troop's work, geography, etc. Distribute them to guests as gestures of good will.

Trips

Find out how things are made. Visit:

- A chocolate, candy-making, or food-processing plant
- A bicycle, motorcycle, or an automobile plant
- A toy manufacturer

OR be adventurous. Visit another time period in history at:

- A Renaissance or historical fair
- A local historic site or event
- A history museum or historic restoration site
- A folk or music festival celebrating arts and music from the past

Activities

Take a trip on a rainy day without leaving your meeting place:

- Transform the indoors into an adventure zone, fantasy island, desert oasis, or three-ring circus.
- Collage a dream vacation by using pictures from travel and geographic magazines. Include everyone's ideas about a perfect spot to visit.

Discussion Topics

What are some of the precautions you need to take when traveling at home and abroad? Who can you go to for help in planning a trip? Where can you get information about places to visit, places to stay, the costs of the trip, the transportation you need to take, and other travel considerations?

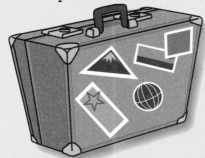

Service Projects

Help younger girls take a journey through a living history program. For descriptions see *www.americangirl.com* or *www.indianjourneys.com* or *www.wolf-ridge.org*. Check out magazines such as *Family Fun*, *Family Life*, and *National Geographic World* for maps and accounts of fun places to visit. Tell younger children or Girl Scouts about these places. Help plan a local trip and accompany them.

It's Great to Be a Girl

Trips

Celebrate being a girl at a place that caters to women's beauty, sponsors women's health, or shows women's power.

- Visit a day spa. Arrange for a donation or discounted treatment, such as a foot massage, hairstyling, or exercise session.

- See how women dressed throughout time by touring a costume shop. Check with local theatrical groups or a school drama department to find out about a shop nearby.

- Emphasize more than beauty and fashion. Visit a local female politician, community leader, or business leader.

Activities

Girls and women have it better today in many ways than their grandmothers did. Or do they? Visit the future or the past by:

- Making a time capsule including girls' wishes and dreams for future generations. At some later date, reveal what was written and see what came true.

- Going to the library to listen to audio tapes reenacting famous women of the past telling their stories.

- Visiting a women's studies center at a nearby school or college. Ask your host to recommend books of interest to your troop.

Discussion Topics

It's great to be a girl. Here are some topics to discuss:

- What's great and what's not so great about being a girl? What's fair and not fair?

- Discuss the word "harassment." What is the difference between being gently teased and harassed? What are examples?

- Do you think all-girl schools are better than co-ed schools? Why or why not? How are they better or worse?

Service Projects

How can you bring attention to causes concerning girls and women? First, be a good reporter and find out about "hot" issues by reviewing news articles, television programs, and movies that portray girls and young women. Which are favorable? Which are not? Write to the media and make suggestions or express your opinions.

Family and Friends

Trips
Make new friends and keep the old! At a nearby park, community center, or other setting, reunite Girl Scout family members, old and new. Invite older Girl Scouts (including adults) to share their experiences and backgrounds in Girl Scouting with your troop or group. Serve a festive picnic meal or refreshment.

Activities
Your network of family and friends is bigger than you think. Brainstorm three lists of friends and family:

- Those who live nearby

- Those who live one to three hours away

- Those who live more than three hours away or in another state or country

Send greetings or holiday cards to a few from each list. Is there one place you would like to visit? Find a friend or family member who can host you and your troop or group or who can suggest a place where your troop can stay.

Discussion Topics
Relationships are not always easy. Discuss one or more of these issues:
- How should household chores in a family be assigned?
- What can you do when two of your friends are angry with each other?
- How can you help a friend whose parents are getting divorced?

Service Projects
Be a home organizer in service to your family. Create baskets for wandering socks, a center for mail and stationery supplies, areas for recycling and clothing giveaways, and recipe files. Check craft Web sites or look in craft magazines for ways to make baskets or to frame photos. Provide one of those services for another family or a neighbor.

How to Stay Safe

Trips

Sometimes seeing is believing when safety is concerned. Visits to the following places might enhance girls' appreciation for safety.

- A modern day-care facility with all the latest safety features

- A car showroom where the salespeople can show and describe the safety features that vehicles are required to have

- Fire or police departments

- American Red Cross offices

Activities

Plan a "Safety Day" event at your school, at a local shopping center or supermarket, or with local Girl Scout troops. Advertise your event. Plan demonstrations in first aid, for example, and skits. Invite guest speakers to be part of the program and invite local organizations concerned with safety issues to distribute pamphlets or brochures.

Discussion Topics

- What constitutes an emergency? When should girls dial 911? When should they call places like the police or fire department?

- How can girls avoid getting into dangerous situations with people they meet on the Internet?

- Should Junior Girl Scouts be allowed to travel alone? At what time of day or night should they be required to come home?

- Who should girls tell if they have a friend who is in trouble, or doing something illegal or unhealthy, like smoking or drinking?

Service Projects

A well-made and properly stocked first aid kit can be a lifesaver. Together with your troop or group, prepare a kit to donate to a day-care facility with limited resources, to a homeless shelter, or to your Girl Scout council who can loan it to other troops for outings.

Be Healthy, Be Fit

Activities

Exercising regularly is one of the best ways for youngsters to stay healthy and fit. Running provides a terrific cardiovascular workout. Have girls host a one mile "fun run" for other girls in Girl Scouting or in the community. Create a T-shirt for participants to wear. Show girls how to use a stopwatch to time the finishers. Girls can celebrate their accomplishment with healthy refreshments after the race.

Service Projects

Have girls host a health and nutrition fair for other kids that showcases the recipes, nutritional advice, and games and sports that they learned from their handbooks.

Trips

Learning about health and fitness can be fun—especially if girls see health and fitness in action in places they may never have thought of. Trips to places like the following can really make the subject come alive.

- A professional sports arena or training facility

- A class on martial arts or yoga

- A working farm, or one that grows organic produce

- A vegetarian restaurant

- A cooking school

Discussion Topics

- Even at 8-11 years of age, Junior Girl Scouts may feel stress because they have too many things to do. Ask them how they can handle all their responsibilities and reduce their stress at the same time.

- What do girls think about women in professional sports? Is there enough representation?

- Do the gym teachers in school treat the boys and girls the same? How do girls feel about this?

Let's Get Outdoors

Trips

Where do the animals roam? birds flock? fish swim? Find and draw them. Explore animal life in at least three places, such as:

- An aquarium or a zoo

- A bird sanctuary or a nature arboretum

- An ocean, lake, or pond

- A nature conservancy, botanical gardens, or a raptor center

- A cider mill, a maple syrup farm, or a beekeeper's station

Activities

Plant a garden or design a rock garden to beautify your environment. You may want to paint and shellac some of the rocks with your names and designs. Look at landscaping and gardening magazines, or books about *feng shui*, a system of improving living space.

Service Projects

Create an outdoor carnival with fitness stations. Invite the public and use admission and ticket-sale money to pay for your props and equipment. Bring your show on the road.

Create and Invent

Discussion Topics

- Do girls think that art must always be beautiful? If yes, who decides how beautiful is defined?

- What kinds of inventions would girls create to help preserve the environment? to help make life easier at school? to assist girls with disabilities?

- In what careers is creativity especially important? Why?

Trips

Creating and inventing occur in lots of common places, and some uncommon ones as well. Some of these trips will reveal creativity at its best.

- Visit the office of an engineer, designer, or architect and ask for a demonstration of a computer-aided design (CAD) program.

- Visit a toy store and look for toys that inspire kids to be creative.

- Visit the studio of a fashion designer.

- Go backstage at a theater, TV studio, or concert hall.

- Attend a crafts fair.

- Go to a trade show in an area of interest to the girls in your troop or group, such as toys, computers, boats, or winter sports.

Activities

Host an "Invention Convention." Many agencies or organizations host competitions where individuals can enter their inventions and win prizes. You can host a similar event for Girl Scouts. You might want to invite people who have created successful inventions to attend or to act as judges if you decide that prizes will be awarded.

Service Projects

Encourage girls to be creative in inventing games, toys, activities, or songs that they can use to inspire creativity in children in a pre-school or day care center. Once they have developed their plans, arrange for them to test their inventions with children on site.

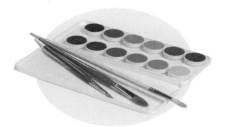

Explore and Discover

Trips

Junior Girl Scouts have such active imaginations and natural energy that exploring and discovering are second nature for them. The following trips might prove exciting for the girls in your troop or group.

- Attend a concert, recital, or musical play. If possible, ask for a tour of the stage.

- Visit a working farm, an apple orchard, or dairy.

- Visit a bread bakery after it has closed for the day. Ask the baker to talk about the tools of the trade and to show how pretzels might be considered a form of bread.

- Enjoy a meal prepared by students at a culinary school.

- Visit a scientist's working laboratory.

Activities

Today, doing business on the Internet is almost as common as shopping at a store. Have the girls in your troop or group create an e-business. Have them consider who their clients would be, how they would stock their products, how they would handle shipping and billing, how they would keep their site current, how they would get their dot.com funded, as well as any other issues they think are important.

Discussion Topics

- In what ways can girls link hobbies and careers?

- How do girls feel about space exploration? Do they think that astronauts will eventually explore beyond the moon?

- How do girls think that the past can help people explore and discover things about the future?

Service Projects

Safety on the Internet is critical for youngsters. Girl Scouts are lucky because they receive safety tips on the "Just for Girls" Web site. Together with your troop or group, create a way to share Internet safety information with other girls who may not be Girl Scouts or who may not have access to the "Just for Girls" Web site.

4 Working with Junior Girl Scouts

Junior Girl Scouts are in the late childhood years of 8 to 11. Those years are filled with activity, intellectual growth, new friendships, deepening relationships, and discoveries both in the outside world and of their inner selves. While family is still very important to the Junior Girl Scout, friends and outside interests and experiences are increasing in importance.

▶ **The Junior Girl Scout is becoming more aware of herself as an individual. In turn, she may be more self-conscious and wonder how others see her.**

Junior Girl Scouts with Special Needs

Many children have some kind of disability. Federal legislation gives all children with disabilities the right to a free and appropriate education designed to meet their individual needs. Disabilities are physical, psychological, cognitive, or arise when health needs affect a person's participation in daily activities.

Girl Scouts is an organization for all girls, and includes members with all kinds of abilities and disabilities. An atmosphere of understanding and acceptance can help children with disabilities discover their abilities, strengths, and gifts and can help all girls appreciate and accept differences.

As the Girl Scout leader, the most important thing you can do is focus on the girl as an individual. Be sensitive to the special needs she has because of her disability, but focus on what she can do rather than what she can't. Involve her in all activities, adapting them when necessary.

For further information on disabilities, as well as specific tips for working with all girls, consult the Girl Scout publication *Focus on Ability: Serving Girls with Special Needs.*

Junior Girl Scouts enjoy learning new skills, particularly ones they can demonstrate. They are also very capable of using their imaginations for both enjoyment and problem solving. Their use of language is growing ever more complex. Girls of this age tend to enjoy codes, riddles, jokes, and puns.

Games for 8-11 year olds can be both imaginative and complex. They should help girls develop new and more demanding skills. These skills can relate to complicated physical activities like gymnastics or to intellectually challenging games like chess.

As the Junior Girl Scout reaches the age of 11, she is entering adolescence. For many girls, the body's hormones have already set in motion the physical changes characteristic of adolescence. It is a time when girls are looking forward with both excitement and apprehension to gaining greater freedom and responsibility, making new friends, and possibly attending a different school.

Questions and Answers About Behavior

During your time as a Girl Scout leader, you will inevitably have to deal with a variety of behavior problems and conflicts with girls.

Q: **What should you do when you hear one girl cursing at another during a troop meeting?**

A: Junior Girl Scouts are at an age when they may want to try out expletives and other inappropriate language they have heard that they are forbidden to use at home. Explain to girls why some terms or words are simply inappropriate and actually offensive. Set expectations. Explain that such language is not acceptable during meetings. Here are some other tips to follow when conflicts arise between girls:

• When a conflict arises between two girls, the best solution is dialogue. Have the girls discuss why they are angry at one another. If they are able, have them resolve to try harder to work toward understanding and appreciating one another.
• Encourage girls to solve their own problems, to go to one another for assistance, and to take turns leading the group. Intervene only if you are really needed. Try to foresee trouble. Step in immediately if anyone's safety is endangered.
• Set limits and make them clear and consistent. Watch for opportunities where girls can participate in rule setting. In many situations, they can help develop and implement rules as well as change them when necessary.

Q: **What should you do if the girls in your troop express interest in a topic in which you have absolutely no experience or expertise?**

A: You are not expected to be all-knowing, even if the girls in your troop think otherwise! As a Junior Girl Scout leader you can teach girls the value of contacting experts in fields you are not familiar with. You may suggest they use trial and error as a method of learning. Use these tips when working on badges or other projects with your troop or group.

• Allow girls to learn by experience. Encourage them to find out things for themselves. Offer help when you feel they may experience failure or discouragement.
• Encourage girls to work on projects in pairs or in groups. Doing activities with friends is a critical part of the Junior Girl Scout experience. Because cliques form easily at this age, try changing the groupings often. Make full use of the buddy system (pairing girls so they can watch out for each other). Rotate buddies so everyone gets a chance to know everyone else.
• Do not expect every girl to participate in all activities. Some girls will not be ready or willing to participate in large-group activities. Gently encourage participation, particularly for girls who are shy, but do not insist upon it. For girls not interested in a particular activity, suggest a quiet activity they can do alone that will not disturb the group.
• Share your successes and resources with other groups, and ask them to share theirs. Ask to observe other troops and groups and see if you can gather some good ideas.

Q: **What should you do when you hear girls in your troop stereotype people who are different from themselves?**

A: In Girl Scouting, "every girl, everywhere" is the theme, so you need to encourage the members of your troop to recognize and value differences in people and cultures. The tips below offer some guidance for accomplishing this goal.

• When you hear girls making negative racial, ethnic, or religious remarks, use those stereotypes as an opportunity to explain that everyone has a unique background, often with a blend of different ethnicities and cultures.
• Make sure girls understand that slurs will not be tolerated at Girl Scout meetings or events. Have them repeat the Promise and Law as an affirmation that they will appreciate others and make sure they understand what they are saying.
• Encourage respect for differing cultural, ethnic, religious, and racial backgrounds. Help each girl express pride in her heritage. Discover ways for girls to learn about and have positive experiences with girls and adults different from themselves.
• Encourage respect for people of differing abilities and for people of different economic backgrounds.

Q: What should you do to increase involvement of parents and guardians in your group?

A: Plan some activities that can only be accomplished with the attendance of a parent or a guardian. A "Special Adult in My Life" dance or a camp-out are two examples. You might also create a schedule at the beginning of the troop year and ask parents or guardians to sign up to co-host one meeting with you.
Here are some other ideas:
- Get a "profile" of parents and guardians at the beginning of the troop year—hobbies, special interests, careers. See how these match up with the troop activities your girls choose to do and ask for assistance in the adult's area of expertise.
- Make sure family members are kept informed about troop activities, not only the special events and trips, but also the day-to-day highlights and activities. Girls can periodically create and bring home their own newsletter that highlights their achievements.
- Try to ensure that there are no barriers to participation by family members: accessibility of a meeting or event site, languages spoken, time of day an event is held, etc. Ask your local Girl Scout council representative for assistance in overcoming barriers.

Q: What if you have an overabundance of family members who are too enthusiastic and overly involved?

A: The leader who is begging for help may shake her head at this question, but it's often feast or famine. Some leaders are inundated with too much participation, allowing little freedom for the girls who may be looking forward to some time just with friends. Or the problem may be one or two family members who always show up with younger children in tow. You don't want to offend anyone, and help is welcome, yet too much might be as big a problem as too little. You may need to stick with a strict participation schedule, rotating participation so that no one family member gets to go more often than others. *Safety-Wise* contains guidelines on the numbers of adults needed to accompany girls on trips and events and on the insurance implications of allowing younger children to tag along. You should also ask your local Girl Scout council representative for assistance in handling difficult or delicate matters.

Q: What should you do if one girl in your troop can't sell cookies because her parents refuse to allow her to participate?

A: Selling cookies is a fundamental part of the Girl Scout program and can offer girls a multitude of educational experiences. However, cookie selling is not a condition of being a Girl Scout. If a girl's parents or guardians do not wish her to participate, their wishes should be honored. The tips below might be helpful in handling any discord that may arise about the Girl Scout cookie sale.
- If a parent or guardian does not want her daughter to sell cookies, perhaps there is another role the girl can fill. For example, she can help sort or distribute the cookie boxes. Or she can help make fliers or posters relating to the sale.
- Explain to girls that each member of the troop or group contributes in her own way. If someone can't participate in the cookie sale, maybe she can take an important role in other ways to support the troop or group. The girl herself might have suggestions about how she can contribute.

5 Tried and True Activities

During your time as a Junior Girl Scout leader, there will be days that you want to plan an activity that is a sure thing. The activities contained in this section provide just the answer. They have been proven to work. Some of the activities are timeless—you may recognize them from your childhood or Girl Scout experience. They have been used again and again simply because they are fun for "every girl, everywhere."

Nature Investigation

Objective: To show girls how many different aspects of nature can be seen in a very small area

Materials: A coat hanger or rope for each girl

Preparation time: 2 minutes

Directions: Girls place on the ground wire coat hangers or pieces of rope shaped into circles. Girls get down close to the ground and examine what they find within their circles. How many different plants do they see? Did they find any insects or earthworms? They can draw, photograph, videotape, or list their discoveries and share them during the meeting.

What's In a Name?

Objective: To allow girls to have fun with words, letters, and spelling

Materials: Paper, pens, magic markers

Preparation time: None

Directions:

1. Have girls write their first names on a piece of paper. If their names are short (fewer than four letters) have them use both first and last names.

2. Have them create a poem using all the letters that appear in their name. For example:

Chicks in the sunshine.
Here comes a fox!
Run, chicks, run!
Into the henhouse
Safe at last.

3. When girls are done, have them share their creations with the others in the troop or group. If girls are having difficulty, they can get help from the group.

Crows and Cranes

Objective: To give girls a chance to run around while helping them learn about nature

Materials: Two pieces of rope to make two goal lines. A list of true or false statements about nature.

Preparation time: 15 minutes

Directions: Form two teams. The teams face each other along two lines which are ten feet apart. Twenty-five feet behind each team is a goal line. The crows are "true." The cranes are "false." The leader makes a statement about nature. If it is true, the crows chase the cranes. Any crane caught before she crosses her own goal line becomes a crow and joins the other side. If the statement is false, the cranes chase the crows. The team with the most players at the end wins.

> **Examples of statements might be:**
> • The earth is flat. (false)
> • Insects have 6 legs. (true)
> • All trees lose their leaves. (false)

The Limbo

Objective: A fun way to get some exercise

Materials: A broom stick, bamboo pole, or rope. A cassette player and tape (preferably the limbo song or Caribbean-style steel drum music).

Preparation time: 1-2 minutes

Directions: Start with two girls holding the limbo stick high in the air. Girls dance to the music as they move under the stick. Encourage girls to lean back instead of forward as they travel under the stick. After each girl has gone under the stick once, the stick is lowered slightly and the girls go again. Continue to limbo under the stick to see who can limbo the lowest.

Look-Alike Cookies

Objective: To show how each girl is different and special in a variety of ways

Materials: A recipe and the ingredients to make gingerbread cookies. Food items to decorate the cookies: gumdrops, raisins, shoelace licorice, and cake decorating icing. A commercial cookie cutter of a gingerbread boy/girl, or one that you make from cardboard.

Preparation time: The time it takes to shop for the ingredients and to locate a recipe

Directions: Make gingerbread dough according to the recipe. Have girls make a cardboard template of a gingerbread person, or use a store-bought cookie cutter.

Note: Make sure the cookie is big enough to decorate with unique features, such as eyeglasses, clothing, and shoes. Each girl cuts out the cookie that she will decorate. After the cookies are baked, the girls decorate the cookies in their own likenesses. They may want to "dress" them in sports uniforms, tutus, tap shoes, parkas, ski outfits, bathing suits, or in any other way they feel is appropriate. Girls might also try to match their physical characteristics, like hair color, length, or texture. Or, they may add things like eyeglasses. Some girls might want to get really creative by making additional props like tennis racquets, skis, or a shopping bag from the leftover dough. Encourage them to be playful and to have fun creating their "doughy" likenesses.

Tried and True Activities

A Special Valentine's Day

Visit a nursing home or senior citizens center

Objective: To enable girls to engage in a philanthropic endeavor that engenders positive feelings in both the girls and the people they visit

Materials: Homemade greeting cards, music

Preparation time: After confirming the place and time of the visit, enough time is needed to create one Valentine's Day card for each individual who will be in attendance when you visit the nursing home or senior citizens center.

Directions: Plan a trip to a nursing home or senior citizens center on Valentine's Day. Have girls create one card for each of the residents that they will visit. Sing, play music, or do skits related to love, the theme of Valentine's Day. After the performance, distribute the cards and spend some time visiting with the residents. Find out ahead of time, if you can, if any of the senior women were ever Girl Scouts and ask if they can share their Girl Scout memories.

Passing the Time

Objective: To keep girls occupied and happy while you travel to your destination

Materials: Pencils and paper, or a laptop computer if one is available

Preparation time: None

Directions: While traveling, pick words from billboards or business signs and create a story. The story can twist, turn, and change as each new word is added. Have girls record the story on the paper or in the computer. When you arrive at your destination, the girls may want to turn their story into a skit.

This activity can be done individually, in pairs, or as a whole group.

Two (or more) Voices are Louder than One

Objective: To show girls that they can make changes if they work together

Materials:
- Large sheets of paper to brainstorm ideas
- Paper to write the petition
- Pens or a computer and printer to produce the document

Preparation Time: The time it takes to brainstorm issues or problems that bother girls and that they have not been able to address acting alone. (For example, they would like to be able to chew gum at school, they would like to have as much sports practice time as the boys, they would like to be able to use the "good" softball field rather than the dilapidated one at the back of the park.)

Directions:

1. Have girls brainstorm ideas for changes they would like to make at school or in their community. Help the girls be as realistic as possible.

2. Help the girls construct a petition that outlines the request and provides specific reasons why the change would be beneficial. Include lines for the signatures of other kids who favor the petition.

3. Once the girls have gathered signatures, help them decide where they should send the petition. For instance, if they have chosen an issue that has to do with life at school, they may want to send their petition to the school board or the superintendent. If the issue has to do with athletic fields or is related to the local parks, they might want to send it to the parks commissioner.

Gobble-It-Up Garden

Objective: To experience the pleasure of gardening and to grow vegetables that the girls can eat

Materials:
- Pots deep enough for healthy roots (one pot for each girl, if possible, or girls can work together in pairs or larger groups)
- Seeds for vegetables of smaller varieties (for example, Tom Thumb carrots or Bibb lettuce; you can ask at a gardening store for other suggestions)
- Prepared soil
- Water
- Clear plastic wrap
- Old newspapers

Preparation Time: The time it takes to purchase the supplies

Directions:

1. Cover your workspace with old newspapers to make clean-up easier.

2. Have each girl choose a vegetable to plant.

3. Fill the pots with the prepared soil, leaving at least an inch at the top.

4. Place the seeds in the pot and then cover them with additional soil. The rule of thumb is to plant seeds about three times as deep as they are wide. This means that tiny seeds only need a little bit of soil sprinkled on top of them.

5. Water the seeds enough to moisten the soil thoroughly, but do not drench them.

6. Cover the pots with the plastic wrap.

7. When the seeds turn into seedlings, move them to a sunny spot and remove the plastic wrap.

8. Make sure to water the plants regularly.

9. Enjoy a taste test with the girls when the vegetables are grown. You might want to combine this with a vegetarian dinner or discussion about nutrition.

Penny Hike

Objective: To add a new twist to hiking

Materials: A penny

Preparation time: 1 minute

Directions: Go for a hike. Girls flip the penny at the intersection of a street or trail. Heads, turn right. Tails, turn left. Continue in this fashion, letting the penny take the girls wherever it chooses. Be sure to keep track of your twists and turns so you all make it home safely!

Family Bingo

Objective: To encourage positive, fun interaction among girls and families. This is a good ice-breaker activity for the beginning of the troop year when family members have been invited to a meeting.

Materials: A bingo-like card with each square containing a description of a skill (plays piano, for example), a hobby (collects coins), or anything else that would be fun to find out about other people

Preparation time: This activity requires some advance preparation time to create questions and copy cards.

Directions: Have girls get to know one another's families better by playing Family Bingo. Supply each participant with a bingo card. Have each card holder go around the room trying to get signatures of family members in the boxes that apply to them. Girls can get bingo either vertically, horizontally, or diagonally.

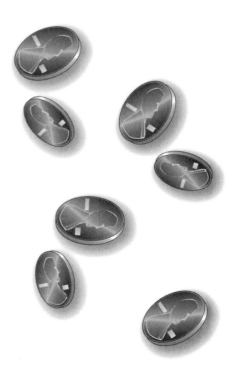

Backwards and Forwards in Engineering

Objective: Word search puzzles are a good way to introduce topics that have a specific vocabulary. It's one tool for girls to explore careers they may not have thought about, such as engineering. Girls can learn jargon related to a subject in a fun manner. (This activity counts toward the "Making It Matter" badge.)

Materials: The puzzle and terms on the next page and the answers on this page.

Preparation time: None

Directions: You can use this word search to introduce the subject of engineering to the girls. You can continue on to more badge activities on this topic, or to a meeting to prepare for a discussion with an engineer who has volunteered to speak about careers.

Engineering Word Search Answers

```
P G U K A F C H E M I C A L N A Y C F M M J W P M
U L T F R X C F Q U B D U G E N O I T A R A P E S
B I O M E D I C A L V O I E N Z E T U C F B C T A
L N S H S B R X A S C S L K G X T J M H K H A R S
I D A C I F C D E P E A E P T D A M X I A E G O M
C U G R S M U K B D C D F R C S I D M N N E L E C
T S N A T D I S T I L L A T I O N R I E J L H E C
R T S E O H T Y T R F C M G L S B C B O D E C U S
A R K S R O T U I T T P P W E E A S R V S C R M A
N I W E U R A O C T W R O C Z L R R E Q D T O I M
S A Q R L N E G L O S E L I B O M O T U A R T T M
P L J I O Z P M V A K F Y G A J P U U R O O C A E
O D E R E A C T O R S B M I N I N G P W R N U L L
R C E P E O H M E N L E E Q A N Y Q M I M I D L E
T A C T I R X W J Q G J R H E L U T O V K C N U C
A V R Y W U O K H M L X I L V O X H C N Z S O R T
T B N S J P A Z F L O G E C N A T I C A P A C G R
I N S T R U M E N T A T I O N C B P K E A P I I I
O R O T A V E L E D H L A Q W P J O M Y F O M C C
N A G W H D M N Y B U I L D I N G S I U L O E A A
O E S N F E I O G C M U J X H S Y G D A P Z S L L
I L P E R G M D R E L E R U T C U R T S A R F N I
E C T J N C V L E O A Y B G A M F B K P A N M O V
E U K E Q U B A N P A R D C M A S S E C O R P R I
E N V I R O N M E N T A L S R M E A I C H E C A C
```

Engineering Associations

AICHE - American Institute of Chemical Engineers (for more information, contact 1-800-AIChemE or 212-591-8100; fax 212-591-8888; e-mail: xpress@aiche.org; Web site: http://www.aiche.org)

ASCE - American Society of Chemical Engineers

ASME - American Society of Mechanical Engineers

IEEE - Institution of Electrical and Electronics Engineers

AIME - American Institute of Mining, Metallurgical and Petroleum Engineers

Find the following engineering terms in the word search.

Main Engineering Disciplines and Related Terms:
Chemical
Electrical
Atom
Capacitance
Distillation
Circuit
Petroleum
Electronics
Polymer

Instrumentation
Process
Laser
Reactors
Resistor
Separation
Semiconductor
Civil
Mechanical
Bridge
Automobiles
Buildings

Elevator
Dam
Engine
Infrastructure
Public Transportation
Roads
Tunnel
Gear
Machine
Power
Pump
Nuclear

Specialty Engineering Disciplines:
Aeronautical
Biomedical
Environmental
Industrial
Metallurgical
Mining
Research

Other Engineering Terms:
Computer
Design
Energy
Extract
Math
Ore

Engineering Word Search

How many engineering terms from the above list can you find?
Look up and down, left and right, and diagonally, either forwards or backwards.

```
P G U K A F C H E M I C A L N A Y C F M M J W P M
U L T F R X C F Q U B D U G E N O I T A R A P E S
B I O M E D I C A L V O I E N Z E T U C F B C T A
L N S H S B R X A S C S L K G X T J M H K H A R S
I D A C I F C D E P E A E P T D A M X I A E G O M
C U G R S M U K B D C D F R C S I D M N N E L L E
T S N A T D I S T I L L A T I O N R I E J L H E C
R T S E O H T Y T R F C M G L S B C B O D E C U S
A R K S R O T U I T T P P W E E A S R V S C R M A
N I W E U R A O C T W R O C Z L R R E Q D T O E I
S A Q R L N E G L O S E L I B O M O T U A R T T M
P L J I O Z P M V A K F Y G A J P U U R O O C A E
O D E R E A C T O R S B M I N I N G P W R N U L L
R C E P E O H M E N L E E Q A N Y Q M I M I D L E
T A C T I R X W J Q G J R H E L U T O V K C N U C
A V R Y W U O K H M L X I L V O X H C N Z S O R T
T B N S J P A Z F L O G E C N A T I C A P A C G R
I N S T R U M E N T A T I O N C B P K E A P I I I
O R O T A V E L E D H L A Q W P J O M Y F O M C C
N A G W H D M N Y B U I L D I N G S I U L O E A A
O E S N F E I O G C M U J X H S Y G D A P Z S L L
I L P E R G M D R E L E R U T C U R T S A R F N I
E C T J N C V L E O A Y B G A M F B K P A N M O V
E U K E Q U B A N P A R D C M A S S E C O R P R I
E N V I R O N M E N T A L S R M E A I C H E C A C
```

Evaluating Troop or Group Activities

Once a month, review the statements in this checklist. If most of your answers are yes, your troop or group has a balanced Girl Scout program experience.

Yes	No	Sometimes	

Girls are having fun.

Yes	No	Sometimes	
☐	☐	☐	• The girls are active in planning and choosing activities.
☐	☐	☐	• The girls talk about "our" troop and activities that "we" did.
☐	☐	☐	• The girls feel free to express their opinions, their likes, and their dislikes.

Your troop is meeting program standards.

Yes	No	Sometimes	
☐	☐	☐	• The girls know and understand the Girl Scout Promise and Law and can talk about the ideals expressed in them.
☐	☐	☐	• The times of activities and meetings and the costs of activities are set so that all girls can participate.
☐	☐	☐	• When you review the Girl Scout program standards, you can point to specific troop/group behaviors that meet these standards.
☐	☐	☐	• You follow the *Safety-Wise* guidelines for all activities you do with the girls.
☐	☐	☐	• The girls show an interest in helping people in their communities and families.

The troop activities are balanced.

Yes	No	Sometimes	
☐	☐	☐	• The activities are varied, not too many of one type. For example, activities would not be varied if many arts and crafts activities or too much badge work was being done.
☐	☐	☐	• Wider opportunities—activities outside the regular troop meeting site—are part of the troop's activities.
☐	☐	☐	• Girls choose activities that introduce them to a wide range of interests.

The group maintains good relationships.

Yes	No	Sometimes	
☐	☐	☐	• Girls listen to each other and respect each other's differences.
☐	☐	☐	• All girls have opportunities to participate. The activities are not dominated by one or more of the girls.
☐	☐	☐	• The girls feel comfortable. They express their opinions and ideas openly.
☐	☐	☐	• Girls are prompt in arriving and the attendance is good.

6 Resource List

The following is a list of resources for leaders and the resources appropriate for Junior Girl Scouts to use in addition to the *Junior Girl Scout Handbook* and the *Junior Girl Scout Badge Book*, which are described in Section 1 of this book.

Essential Resources for Leaders

Focus on Ability, 1998.

Safety-Wise, 2000.

Junior Girl Scout Handbook, 2001.

Junior Girl Scout Badge Book, 2001.

Issues for Girl Scouts

Connections for Junior Girl Scouts, 1997.

Girls Are Great! for Junior Girl Scouts, 1997.

Media Know-How for Junior Girl Scouts, 1999.

Read to Lead for Junior Girl Scouts, 1997.

Special Interest Books

Ceremonies in Girl Scouting, 1990.

Fun and Easy Nature and Science Investigations, 1996.

Fun and Easy Activities—Nature and Science, 1996. / *Actividades divertidas y fáciles—naturaleza y ciencia*, 1996. (English and Spanish language in same booklet)

Games for Girl Scouts, 1990.

Girl Scout Girl Power! booklet and patch: "Girl Power: How to Get It."

Girl Scouts Against Smoking.

Go Global! Girl Scouts Take a Closer Look at the World.

Junior Girl Scouts Sports Diary, 1997.

Octavia's Girl Scout Journey: Savannah 1916, 1999.

Off and Running: Exploring Sports Careers.

Outdoor Education in Girl Scouting, 1996.

Sing and Dance Around the World!, 1998.

Strength in Sharing: Philanthropy in Girl Scouting, 2000.

Index